POCKET GUIDE TO
Native Americans

WESTHORP & COLLINS

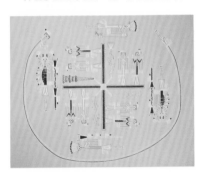

POCKET GUIDE TO
Native Americans

WESTHORP & COLLINS

CRESCENT BOOKS
New York • Avenel, New Jersey

©1993 Salamander Books Ltd.,
129-137 York Way,
London N7 9LG,
United Kingdom.

This 1993 edition published by Crescent Books,
distributed by Outlet Book Company, Inc.,
a Random House Company, 40 Engelhard Avenue,
Avenel, New Jersey 07001

ISBN 0-517-08653-0

8 7 6 5 4 3 2 1

Credits
Authors and editors: Christopher Westhorp and
Richard Collins
Designer: Jane Molineaux
Filmset: The Old Mill, London

Color reproduction: P&W Graphics PTE Ltd, Singapore
Printed in Belgium by Proost International Book Production

Consultant
Jeanne Eder, who wrote the Preface and acted as
consultant to the authors, is an enrolled member of the
Sioux tribe and lives in Dillon, Montana. She has an MA
degree in history from Montana State University (where
she majored in North American Indian history) and is
currently a Ph.D. student in history at Washington State
University.

Picture credits
With the exception of the following, all the photographs
in this book are published with the permission of the
National Anthropological Archives, Smithsonian
Institution, Washington, DC. Front cover and half-title:
Salamander Books; 2–3, 5: ©Buffalo Bill Historical
Center, photography by Devendra Shrikhande; 8: Arizona
Historical Society Library, Tucson; 9: National Archives;
13, 25, 37: Salamander Books; 39: Pitt Rivers Museum,
Oxford; 49: Salamander Books; 57: National Archives;
61: Salamander Books.

Contents

PREFACE, by Jeanne Eder

The year 1992 marked the 500th anniversary, or quincentenary, of Columbus's voyage to the Americas. One could surmise from the celebrations that took place that the attitudes of the dominant culture have changed little and that the education of the last 500 years has not included the realities of the effects of colonization on the indigenous peoples of the Americas.

For the Native Americans the idea of celebrating this event has brought up painful memories of past oppression and strengthened the desire to preserve their own traditional cultures. This preservation has taken many forms; it means that the Native Americans will continue to resist assimilation, and many will not be celebrating events but educating the public to past aggressions and promoting the need to go beyond such mind set.

The Indian people of the United States are considered semi-sovereign. If this means that they do not have the right to negotiate with any foreign power except the United States, it also means that the Federal Government's responsibility is to look after and protect the rights of Indians. However, when one looks at the court cases which end in favor of the Indian nations it is obvious that federal protection occurs only when it is convenient for the government. It is worth observing that they only recognize 381 of the 600-plus Indian nations.

The recent Oscar-winning movie "Dances with Wolves" has created a positive awareness of the Indian people's history. A new sensitivity to the plight of indigenous people has emerged and yet it is not enough. Non-Indian people need to be educated as to the legal rights of the Indian people of the United States and other American countries. Indian people are still in a struggle over the exploitation of their lands and natural resources. They are having to pay lawyers to do their fighting, and winning, in the courtrooms of the United States. And while the interest in them fluctuates, they remain the poorest minority in the United States.

The traditional Indian people have grown up with a belief that they are caretakers of the land and that they must live in harmony with it. Environmentalists throughout the Americas have sought to revive this Indian philosophy in order to bring issues to the forefront. The fact that this has made "Indian-ness" fashionable is an inevitable by-product. The issues are numerous: there are threatened sacred burial and vision quest sites; the repatriation issue of returning the bones of deceased ancestors, yet not returning the burial goods which occupy so many museum shelves; the matters of air, water and noise pollution; and the issues of hunting and fishing rights, wilderness designation, and the preservation of forested lands.

Once again Indian people are finding themselves in the midst of cultural conflict as they struggle to be free of poverty and to develop economic opportunities while attempting not to avoid their traditions. Non-Indian people must reach out and support Indian rights to self-determination by demanding that their tax dollars not be used to dump toxic wastes on Native American lands and by helping the Indians maintain pride in a cultural heritage so important to all of us.

INTRODUCTION

The tribes or nations of the Indian peoples of North America are generally arranged into a number of culturally distinct areas. There are eight areas in this book, as shown in the map (right): North East (1), South East (2), Plains (3), South West (4), California (5), Basin (6), Plateau (7), and North West (8). Although this book concentrates primarily on Indians of the United States, in some cases the more northerly of these groupings cross well into what is now Canada, while the southern ones sometimes cross into Mexico. (Regrettably, lack of space precludes the inclusion of peoples from the outer reaches of the Arctic and Sub-Arctic.) Traditional tribal boundaries preceded the founding of these modern nation states and the establishment of often arbitrary political borders. These borders still present problems for peoples such as the Blackfeet and Mohawk in the north, for example.

It is not known how many tribes have become extinct since European settlers arrived on American shores but it must be hundreds, for in terms of numbers the reduction due to disease, forcible removal and warfare was as high as 95 per cent. Many of these tribes are now lost to history and do not feature in this guide which concentrates mainly on tribes which survive, in varying states of health, into the present.

This book touches on many different aspects of Native American life, such as language, warfare, domestic lifestyle and economy, art and craft, religion, material culture, battles, treaties, and outstanding individuals and leaders. But not everything can be included. The guide should therefore be used as a stepping stone to a broader reading list.

ABENAKI
North East
An important village-based tribe of the powerful Algonquian language family, active in the fur trade, and living in New Hampshire and Maine around the Androscoggin, Kennebee, Penobscot and Saco rivers. There were two main groups, western and eastern, but most withdrew to Canada to ally with the French — where they were known as St Francis Indians. The Abenaki sometimes allied with the Maliseet and were known as the Wabenaki. This may account for some records which state that Abenaki was a collective name for the Maliseet, Micmac, Penobscot and Passamaquoddy. (Some tribes also referred to the Delaware as Wabenaki.) The Abenaki were heavily involved in wars with the New England settlers but did sign a peace treaty in 1699. They were later present among Indians resisting whites in the Ohio River country in the 1730s. It is thought they became extinct.

Right: *Apache scouts like these were vital to the success of Crook's Arizona campaign in the winter of 1872-3 — indeed 10 won Medals of Honor.*

ACCOMAC
North East
These people are little known although it is thought they were relatives of the Powhatan, the powerful Algonquian confederacy which was the first to go to war with the English Virginian settlers in 1622.

ACHUMAWI
California
Also called the Ajumawi or "River People" they lived in Round Valley, northern California, and spoke a Hokan dialect.

Known for their basketry, today they and their kin are known as the Pit River Indians. Their kin the Atsugewi live near their ancestral territory in Lassen National Park, California.

ALABAMA
South East
In 1704 the Alabama numbered less than 1,000; after 1763 they dispersed, some joining the Seminoles and Creeks, most going to Texas with the Koasatis/Coushatta, with whom they shared a similar language, of the

Muskogean family. By 1910 there were about 300 Alabamas, including those among the Creeks.

ALGONQUIAN
North East

A tribe of Maliseet, or Malecite, origin which lived in the Ottowa and Gatineau River valleys of Quebec, cultivating wild rice and growing tobacco. They lent their name to the largest group of linguistically related tribes in North America which held most of the land east of the Mississippi. These foes of the Iroquois

were middlemen in the fur trade and pro-French friends of the Huron. Probably their closest relatives were the Chippewa. Their secret curing society, the Midewiwin, and their highest god, Manitou, are well known. They became acculturated but were never deported.

ALSEANS
North West

Pacific coast-dwelling neighbors of the Tillamook, Siuslawans and Kalapuyans and one of many tribes living off the wealth of the sea.

APACHE
South West

A southern Athapaskan group and relative newcomers to the southwest who lived a semi-nomadic existence, the name Apache applies to a number of tribes all linguistically related. Inhabitants of New Mexico and Arizona, the Apache can generally be divided into eastern and western groups. These groups include, among others, in the east the Jicarilla, Mescalero, Lipan and Chiricahua; in the west the White Mountain, San Carlos, Fort Apache, Pinal, Arivaipa, Apache Peaks, Mazatzal, Tonto and Cibecue. Resistors of Spanish influence up to the 1830s (and raiders into Mexico), thereafter they concentrated their efforts on the United States and their resistance to the whites was among the last offered by Indians in North America. Among those who were the last to capitulate, Cochise and Naiche are legendary figures of the Chiricahua, as was Geronimo who only surrendered in 1886 after forty years of resistance.

Left: *Geronimo (bottom, third from right) and other resisting Chiricahua Apaches, including Naiche (bottom, center), en route to imprisonment in Florida.*

APALACHEE
South East
Speakers of the Muskogean language. Perhaps 5,000 strong in the 17th century, they were greatly reduced in the 18th by English and Creek raids, a few survivors ultimately joining the Creeks. The Carolina slave traders preyed on their Spanish missions, carrying many into the slave markets.

APALACHICOLA
South East
Hitchiti speakers who lived on the borders of modern Alabama, Georgia and Florida; it is said that peace between them and the Muskogee began the Creek confederacy, which arose in the late 17th century.

ARAPAHO
Plains
Algonquian speakers, allied to the Cheyenne, the Arapaho now live on reservations in Oklahoma and in Wyoming. In 1865, along with Kiowa, Comanche and Cheyenne, they ceded land to the US Government at the Council of the Little Arkansas. During the Civil War, militarization of the West took place. The US Government completed many treaties with Indian tribes with the objective of confining Indians to reserved lands. Thereafter they faced the onslaught of Euro-American settlers in their new lands in Kansas and in Indian Territory. The Medicine Lodge Treaty of 1867 further reduced their lands. By 1875 many of their leaders arrested, imprisoned or deported, the Arapaho of the southern plains were on reservations, where they remained, there to regroup for future battles in federal courts.

Above: *Arapaho women confined to the reservation in Oklahoma perform the Ghost Dance religion's Circle Dance in the belief that they will invoke a miraculous return to better days.*

Right: *Black Fox, Arikara warrior. Note the necklace of otter skin and grizzly bear claws. The bear was very powerful "medicine", being highly respected for its wisdom, as well as its strength.*

ARIKARA
Plains

A semi-sedentary tribe, farmers and earth lodge dwellers living on the Upper Missouri River, the Arikara (also known as Ree) were Caddoan speakers

like their southern relatives the Pawnees. They were signatories of the 1851 Fort Laramie Treaty which defined tribal boundaries. Arikara scouts accompanied Custer's Black Hills, Dakota Territory, expedition in 1874.

ASSINIBOIN
Plains

Split from the Yanktonai Sioux, these Nakota speakers — whose name is Ojibwa for "One Who Cooks with Stones" — moved west to ally with the Cree and then fight against the Sioux and Blackfeet. They lived west of Lake Winnipeg, along the Assiniboine and Saskatchewan rivers. Great buffalo hunters they traded pemmican for guns and white's goods. Co-existing with the whites they were hit by smallpox in the 1820s and 1830s but survive today 5,000-strong in Canada (as the Stoney) and the USA.

ATSINA
Plains

An offshoot of the Arapaho, these Algonquian speakers and allies of the Blackfeet were also given the name of Gros Ventre, a mis-translation by the French of their name in sign language.

The tribe was prominent in the development of the fur trade on the northern plains, and the warfare due to it. They were sun-dancers and later settled with the Assiniboin at Fort Belknap in Montana where they numbered 2,000.

Above: *Kill Spotted Horse, warrior of the Assiniboin. The headdress identifies the tribe because of its use of distinctly flat eagle feathers in the center at the top. Note the bone and brass decorations.*

BELLA BELLA
North West

Wakashan speakers from near King Island close to Queen Charlotte Sound. They were also called the Heiltsuk and included the Haihais. Their art was similar to the more northerly Haida.

BELLA COOLA
North West

Salishan speakers culturally similar to their Heiltsuk and Kwakiutl neighbors. Also known as the Nuxalk they used wood for housing, clothes, baskets and totem poles. Their village life was based on hereditary rank and oral tradition was strong. Today they number 1,000.

BILOXI
South East

These Siouan speakers from Mississippi called themselves "First People", as did many other tribes. A small group of 160 or so keeps the name alive today with the Tunica in Louisiana.

BLACKFEET
Plains

Algonquian-speaking, this tribe moved onto the north west plains from the east and ranged over a large stretch of ter-

Above: *Blackfeet warriors early this century. The erect eagle feather headdress is traditional Blackfeet design. Note the sacred painted tipi in the background, again typical of the tribe.*

ritory with the Rocky Mountains behind them. Unrelated to the Teton Sioux band of Blackfoot, their name derives from their moccasins blackened by either paint or the burnt prairie. They soon mastered the horse-culture nomadicism of the plains and, once armed, grew into a powerful, well-led confederacy of sub-tribes totaling 15,000 and embracing the Siksika (Blackfeet proper), Blood (Kainah), and Piegan (Pikuni), with later allies in the Sarcee.

The Blackfeet were hostile to the Plateau and plains' tribes and the Crow, who were all about them, and were central to the fur trade — a fact which led to a state of war with American Fur Co. trappers. They lived in tipis, some of them elaborately painted with pictographs of real and mythical creatures. A sacred painted tipi was a sign of high social standing and it depicted the medicine of a man's dreams. Their decline began in earnest with the smallpox epidemic of 1837 which killed one-third. The decimation of the buffalo was the final blow and in 1883-4 some 600 Piegan starved to death during "Starvation Winter". Today some 7,000 live in Montana (mostly Piegan) and 3,000 in Canada.

APACHE

The artifacts pictured here belong to the Western Apache group at San Carlos and were collected early this century. The main feature seen here is the double saddle bag made of decorated leather with red flannel laid behind the cutwork. The rope which runs across it is made from horsehair. The baskets and water jars (top right) are fine examples of their kind. The ceremonial hat (top, center) is decorated with owl feathers; the war club (top left) is a buckskin sheathed stone attached to a wooden handle.

(American Museum of Natural History, NY)

CADDO
South East

These agriculturalists and skilful potters gave their name to a language group. They lived in conical houses thatched with grass or bark situated along the Lower Red River, in what is now Arkansas and Louisiana, but were pushed south by whites, eventually being forced onto a Washita River reservation. They were organized into bands (Hasinai, Eyeish, Cahinnio, Adai, and others) and were notable for their nose rings and tattoos. They played a key role in early horse trading.

CAHITA
South West

A generic term for Yaqui, Mayo, Tehecua, Sinaloa, Zuaque and other rancheria groups related by language.

CAHOKIA
South East

Part of the Illinois confederacy, the "Wild Geese" lived on the upper Mississippi and are famed for their large flat-topped mounds so typical of a cultural period from AD 1000 to 1200. Their hierarchical society of all-powerful chiefs was similar to the Mexican societies.

Above: *A Catawba man in supposedly traditional wear for a medicine show in 1899. The beaded vest and headdress, however, are both non-Catawba.*

CAHTO
California

Athapaskan speakers from the Cahto valley in California, their culture is close to the Pomo. They are found now at the Laytonville Rancheria.

CAHUILLA
California

Also called the Kawia, these Aztec-Tanoan speakers lived in adobe houses or wall-less lean-tos in a diverse region of desert near the San Gorgonio Pass and San Jacinto mountains. Skilled potters and basket makers, some 1,900 survive today in a number of missions.

CALUSA
South East

These numerous and fierce south west Floridans lived in wooden houses on piles. Able seamen of dugout canoes, they sailed to Cuba and the Caribbean to trade, and either emigrated there in the mid-18th century in the face of Creek and English pressure or were later transported with the Seminole to Oklahoma. They killed Ponce de Leon in 1521 and are notorious for the practice of the chief marrying his full sister.

CATAWBA
South East

This once-large tribe from the Carolinas spoke a Siouan-like tongue. They lived in bark-covered cabins, grew crops, and were called Flatheads by the whites with whom contact brought disease and reduction from 5,000 to 500. Their traditional enemies were the Iroquois (who absorbed some of them). They aided the colonial revolt and live today at Rock Hill, South Carolina, where they still employ the ancient pottery techniques used by their ancestors.

CAYUGA
North East
They called themselves "People of the Mucky Land" and this Iroquoian tribe from central New York state sided with Britain during the Revolution, causing many to flee to Canada afterwards. They lived in extended family groups in longhouses, men hunting and women farming. Today perhaps 400 live among the Seneca in New York, a further 1,500 live on Six Nations Reserve in Ontario, some with the Oneida in Wisconsin, and there are 100 in Oklahoma with the Seneca of Sandusky (a group mixed from Seneca and Mingo).

CAYUSE
Plateau
This Sahaptin-speaking tribe from eastern Washington and Oregon was famed for its breeding of a small horse also known today as a mustang. So important was the horse to them that each person might have 50 or more compared to the horse-wealthy Crow's 15 per lodge. They were ravaged by smallpox in 1847 and merged with the Nez Perce.

CHAKCHIUMA
South East
They were absorbed by the Chickasaw and Choctaw in the 17th century.

CHATOT
South East
By 1817 they had vanished, having been pushed from their homelands to Mobile Bay in modern-day Louisiana.

CHEHALIS
North West
A small group of Coast Salish stock who originate from the Chehalis River area. Lewis and Clark met them in 1806 and today there are some 700 registered on their reservation at the Olympic Peninsula Agency in Washington.

Right: *A typical Cayuse rush-mat covered dwelling. The women wear hats and patterned buckskin dresses — good examples of their fine costumes.*

CHEMEHUEVI
Basin

An isolated group of Paiute Shoshonean speakers, this tribe lived in small bands as hunters and gatherers along the Colorado River. Their lifestyle was similar to the Mohave and the tribe was notable for excellent basketry. A few live today on a reservation of that name, plus 100 more on a small territory astride the California/Arizona border.

CHERAW
South East

Of eastern Siouan stock they were hostile to colonists and were extinct by 1760 as an independent group, but their blood lives on in the Lumbee.

CHEROKEE
South East

Once one of the great tribes of Tennessee, Virginia and the Carolinas, today's Cherokee are mostly found in Oklahoma (95,000), descendants of those transported along the infamous "Trail of Tears" in 1838/39. Some 10,000 Eastern Cherokee still live on their historic lands (at Qualla Reservation), descendants of those who hid in the Smoky Mountains. The Cherokee speak

a strain of Iroquoian, having been pushed out of the Great Lakes area by the Delaware and Iroquois. Their culture — with the exception of the hereditary principle — came to resemble the Creeks and they lived in log cabins in red (war) and white (peace) towns, each with a supreme chief and a central hall for debating. They ceded large amounts of land to the British in 1773 and 1775. After the Revolution American encroachment saw massive loss of land and pressure to assimilate. They tried to accommodate, becoming literate, adopting a written constitution, and even helping to fight the Creek, but it was not enough to stop further white designs on their

Above: *The Cherokee Ballplayers' Dance at Qualla Reservation. A woman beats a drum and a man shakes a gourd rattle while the players circle anti-clockwise, with their sticks, around a small fire.*

land. The Cherokee signed 40 treaties in total — all broken. The Indian Removal Act of 1830 went ahead under President Jackson, their ally in the Creek War, despite the Supreme Court having ruled for the Cherokee. The federal government had promised Georgia in 1702 that it would free the state of its Indians. The survivors (one-quarter died en route) joined the Creek,Chickasaw, Choctaw and Seminole.

CHEYENNE
Plains

These Algonquian farmers and potters from Minnesota were pushed on to the high plains by the expanding Sioux in about 1750. Their name derives from the Sioux term "Sha-hi'-ye-na" meaning "people of alien speech". By the 1830s they owned horses and had become typical nomadic plainsmen, hunting the buffalo and antelope. They also split into two groups, one at the Platte River's headwaters, the other moving south along the Arkansas River. The Treaty of Fort Laramie in 1851 formalized this split into Northern and Southern branches. Deeply religious, their cosmic outlook included a Universe that was connected to various symbolic points. Thus they prayed to the directions, the Sky Father and the Earth Mother. They also stressed supernatural warrior visions and with the Arapaho they were probably the most complete practitioners of the sun dance. Uniquely, they carried tribal sacred bundles into battle as a talisman: that of the Southern Cheyenne was called the "Sacred Arrows", and that of the Northern Cheyenne the "Sacred Medicine Hat" bundle. The arrows are still occasionally in use today.

Above: *A Cheyenne warrior, his long braids decorated with several eagle feathers. The style is personal and based on his appearance in dreams and visions.*

A well-organized tribe, they had 10 major bands with 44 chiefs appointed for wisdom or valor, among the most famous of whom were Dull Knife, Little Robe, Two Moons and Little Wolf. Four chiefs were selected to be the principals.

Despite their strength they were never a numerous tribe and at their height numbered only 3,500 (cholera had taken its toll in 1849). The Northern were active against the white settlers and took part in the Bighorn action of 1876. Their Southern kin did not wage war in earnest until after Black Kettle's village had been attacked in Colorado in 1864 and on the Washita in 1868 — despite their having signed the Medicine Lodge Treaty in 1867. They then joined the Comanche-led uprisings of 1874-5. Sweet victories could not disguise the fact that faced by overwhelming numbers and weaponry, and with the buffalo destroyed, the plains Indians were broken. Militarily undefeated, the Cheyenne were confined to reservations and today there are 4,500 living on the Tongue River in Montana and several thousand with the Arapaho in Oklahoma.

CHICKAHOMINY
North East

An Algonquian tribe in the conquest state presided over by Powhatan. Today they are the largest Indian group in Virginia and still function as a tribe with a chief. They live on both sides of the river they are named after.

CHICKASAW
South East

Of Muskogean linguistic stock these semi-nomads inhabited the border area of Mississippi and Alabama. They lived in scattered riverside settlements and, with French help, they raided northwards, taking captives. Although speaking the same language as the Choctaw they sided with Britain against them and the French. They opposed the Revolution and were later removed from their territory with other tribes and taken to Oklahoma. During the Civil War they sided with the Confederacy and not just out of hope for the return of their lands. It was an irony that many Chickasaw chiefs by this time were mixed-bloods owning slaves and cotton plantations. Victory was not to be and they remain in Oklahoma numbering 6,000.

CHINOOK
North West

This tribe lived along the lower Columbia River and were famed traders as a result of their rich salmon rivers. As a result their language became trading jargon far and wide, and from it comes "potlatch" meaning "to give". Lewis and Clark first encountered them in 1805 in

their elaborately carved canoes. Naturally, they held potlatches but were notable for basing religion around the salmon's annual run.

CHIPPEWA
North East

This major group of the Algonquian family was also known as the southern Ojibwa (the northern were the Nipissing and Mississauga) and were really a closely related trio of Ojibwa, Ottawa and Potawatomi. They lived in the forests

Above: *This Chippewa dwelling is typical of Great Lakes' tribes. It is a dome framed with saplings and covered with tree bark, mainly birch, and reed mats.*

on Lake Huron's shores and grew with the fur trade. They also had groups further west with the Cree known as the Salteaux, and on the plains as the Bungi. They were warriors of some stature and drove the Sioux out of Minnesota, creating enmity lasting 200 years. Their last battle was against the

US Army and took place at Leech Lake in 1898 — some eight years after Wounded Knee. (This was the last armed conflict of the Indian Wars.)

Chippewa culture had many of the core elements of that of the woodland people: the Feast of the Dead ceremonial; the Grand Medicine or Midewiwin curatives; a fear of sorcery; and a large stock of destructive spirits and supernatural beings in the natural world. They were famed for their use of birch bark which formed the basis of their culture, and were excellent canoe makers and caribou hide tanners. Large reservations in North Dakota and Minnesota host 20,000 today.

CHITIMACHA
South East

Once the most powerful tribe on the northern gulf coast west of Florida, this Muskogean related language group included the Washa and Chawasha tribes and had a rigid social structure with hereditary leadership. Their tattooed warriors lost a long war with the French in the 18th century and many were enslaved. Even so some 400-odd still live today near Grand Lake, Louisiana.

Below: *Toshkachito, a Choctaw from Louisiana, shoots a cane blowgun. The wooden dart was feathered with thistle down. Its effective range was 25ft (7.6m).*

CHOCTAW
South East

Possibly descended from the Chickasaw, these people were the largest Muskogean group and lived along the Chickasawhay, Pearl and Pascagoula rivers. Highly skilful Mississippean farmers they produced a crop surplus with which to trade. They lived in mud-plastered, thatched log cabins and eventually left their territory due to the white settler's desire for cotton lands. They were caught up in the wars of the competing colonial powers which raged in their lands, but remained on good terms with the Americans — even fighting for them against the Creek in 1811. This friendship did not spare them when the time for removal came. (One macabre aspect of their lives was the ritual bone-picking of the dead by professionals with special tattoos and long fingernails.) They were forced to relocate to the west in 1830 when a minority of their leaders were bribed into signing the Treaty of Dancing Rabbit Creek. Some (5,000) resisted deportation and still live on a reservation in Mississippi — with others in Louisiana — but most (34,000) live in Oklahoma where they keep alive the Green Corn festival.

CHOWANAC
South East

A large tribe from what is now North Carolina, these were the most important Algonquians south of the Powhatan. They warred with the colonists in 1663 and 1675 and were confined to a reservation in 1707, probably joining the Tuscarora later.

CHUMASH
California

This populous Hokan-speaking tribe of skilled artisans lived in domed communal houses along the California coast from Malibu to Estero Bay and three offshore islands. They had seven major groups, five of them taking their names from Franciscan missions. Nearly 1,000 live now on the Santa Ysabel Reservation in California.

CLACKAMAS
North West

One of 14 tribes forming a confederation at Grande Ronde in Oregon.

Right: *These Cocopa males in breechclouts were pictured aboard the vessel* Narragansett *in 1874. The tribal culture spurned material wealth.*

CLALLAM
North West

The "Strong People" are a Salish tribe on the south side of Puget Sound and Vancouver Island. They are related to the Songish.

COCHIMI
South West

Hokan-speaking lowland Yumans living along the Colorado River.

COCOPA
South West

A Hokan-speaking lowland Yuman group of rancheria culture whose cultural antipathy to personal wealth and goods stemmed from their living close to a river subject to periodic flooding and high risk of loss of any belongings. They live today, some 700 in all, at Sumerton, in the state of Arizona.

COEUR D'ALÊNE
Plateau

Named as the "Awl Heart" by a French trader, they are also known as the Skitswish. They spoke Interior Salish and lived in Idaho and Washington. They hunted on the plains in Crow and Blackfeet country. Today about 800 live on their reservation with the Nez Perce in Idaho and others at Colville.

COLUSA
California

A tiny rancheria group reduced to less than 100 today.

COLVILLE
Plateau

Taking their name from a Hudson Bay fort, these Salishan speakers lived in the Washington/Idaho area and fished along the Columbia — especially for salmon at Kettle Falls. Today they live on the Colville Reservation, Washington, as one of the Confederated Tribes numbering some 4,000 people. With the exception of a few Nez Perce, the others are all Salish: Coeur d'Alêne, Entiat/Chelan, Kalispel, Methow, Nespelem, Okanagan, Palus, Sanpoil, Senijextee and Spokane.

COMANCHE
Plains

These superb horsemen and horse-breeders were highly feared raiders as far south as Durango in Mexico. They called themselves Nemenuh or "The People", but the word Comanche is derived from the Ute word Komántcia meaning "Anyone who wants to fight me all the time". Of Uto-Aztecan linguistic stock, they began as part of Wyoming's Shoshoni but moved south, displacing the Apache and setting a pattern of aggressive activity that was to see them defend the high plains near the Arkansas

Above: *Quanah Parker and his wife Tonasa after he had adopted certain ways of the whites. His name meant "fragrant", but it is as a fierce warrior protecting his people that he is remembered.*

River against all-comers for the best part of 150 years.

The tribe had perhaps 12 autonomous bands, five of them major: Honey-Eaters (Pehnatekuh), Antelope (Kweharehnun), Those-Who-Turn-Back (Nawkoni), Yap- or Root-Eaters (Yamparikuh), and Buffalo-Eaters (Kutsuehka). Aware of the dangers from white expansion, they organized a tribal united front (The Great Peace) and attacked settlers from 1834 onward led by Ten Bears, Kicking Bird (Kiowa) and Quanah Parker. Their hatred was strongest for Texans: in 1840 they had 12 of their chiefs murdered by them during peace talks. The US government tried to secure lasting peace at Medicine Lodge Creek in 1867 but in 1868 Sheridan ordered free tribes to surrender or be hunted. Many did, including Ten Bears, and Parker's group formed most of those left on the Staked Plains. Their 40-year resistance, however, was not enough and the reservation awaited them and their Kiowa allies in 1875. Their beliefs were mainly individual and group rituals few until the peyote cult spread, helped by Quanah Parker who tried to help his people adapt after their defeat. They have survived, numbering 5,000 in Oklahoma.

CONCHO
California

A typical rancheria tribe from south east Arizona and New Mexico.

CONOY
North East

An Algonquian tribe from Baltimore, Maryland, also called the Piscataway and associated with the Delaware and Nanticoke who they had moved north to mix with and among whom some still claim descent.

COOS
North West

Still located in the Coos Bay area on the central coast of modern-day Oregon, the Coos have been part of a confederation with the Siuslaw and Umpqua since 1853. They were at one time transported but they returned and are notable for having been "terminated" as a tribe in 1956 against their will and then "restored" in 1984. The three total less than 300 today.

COSTANOAN
California

Penutian speakers, these people lived originally in the San Francisco Bay area

Above: *A Cree hunting camp, possibly in Hudson Bay where they were often called Swampy Cree. Note the canoes at the ready nearby. The poles offer protection from the strong, destructive winds.*

and southwards but were dispersed by the Mexicans. They had eight major subdivisions and were often referred to as the "Ohlone" for a common identity. They ate the staple acorn and hunted wildlife. They wore striped tattoos and sometimes mud for insulation. Their village groups became fodder for the Franciscan missions and culture and race became so diluted that the few remaining have a task to rebuild.

COUSHATTA
South East

Originally from the east they were pushed west from Alabama and live now in Texas mixed with the tribe of Alabama. A number (300) also live in Louisiana.

CREE
North East/Plains

A major Algonquian group, the Cree are one of the great Indian peoples and exist in two groups: the Woodland and Plains. They expanded from their James Bay base as a result of the fur trade and their acquisition of guns. War and smallpox contained them but they still number 70,000 today across North

America. Religion and ceremony were valued highly and as hunters it is no surprise to find their culture full of respect for animals and natural spirits. The bear in particular was a highly honored animal due to its power and way of life. The Cree stories consider the winds to be four brothers, the oldest and most powerful one being North. On the plains their traditional allies were the Assiniboin. The Cree also intermarried with Europeans to create a large mixed-race culture known as the Métis.

CREEK
South East

A tribe in upper (Muskogee) and lower (Hitchiti and Alabama) groups which occupied huge expanses of what are now Georgia and Alabama. (Some Lower Creek emigrated to Florida, becoming the Seminole or "separatists".) The Creek rose to prominence in the late 17th century. Their stratified society was based on merit. Towns were social and political units (in red/war and white/peace groups) and formed the democratic base of their union. (The red/white affiliation was not permanent and could be changed by defeat in a stick-ball game.) They are organized into towns to this day. They built their houses around plazas and raised temples on mounds. The central festival was the annual poskita or Green Corn Ceremony.

They sold a lot of their land to the English, but after the Revolution more was wanted and in 1813 the half-Creek Shawnee chief Tecumseh roused support among the Creeks for war with the US. Civil war among the Creeks followed, with militant Red Sticks under Minawa taking up the fight against pro-US Creeks, Cherokees and Choctaw led by the mixed-blood McIntosh fighting for Jackson and crushing Minawa's forces at Horseshoe Bend. Harsh terms followed for the defeated, and the only Creek that live today in their homeland are a small group (1,000) in south Alabama allowed to stay by Jackson as reward for their part in his victory. The remainder (50,000) are in Oklahoma.

Below: *George W. Stidham and his family. He is a typical mixed-blood Creek aristocrat and Southern slave owner.*

CROW
Plains

This Siouan-speaking people gave themselves a bird name "Apsaruke", meaning "Children of the Large Beaked Bird", later mis-translated as "Crow". They were linguistically-related to the Hidatsa but moved west to the Yellowstone and its Powder, Bighorn and Wind valleys. They were highly skilled raiders and their warriors were honored for capturing horses, making them the Sioux's main enemy (unlike their Dakota enemies, the Crow favored unpainted tipis). When they departed from the Hidatsa, their leader No Vitals was instructed in a dream to plant tobacco. Thus the Tobacco Society was created to supervise the planting of this gift. The crop played a central part in tribal life and was considered sacred.

The men wore elegant long hair, dressed well, and the tribe itself was known far and wide for their robe making and decorative skills. They had three bands — Mountain (Acaraho), River (Minesepere) and Kicked-in-Their-Bellies (Erarapio) — and possessed a number of military societies, notably the Lumpwoods. Their famous chiefs included Medicine Crow and Plenty Coups. It was a Crow claim that they had never killed a white man except in self-defense. Their scouts served the US Army during the wars against the Sioux and they were serving in their homeland with Custer's 7th Cavalry when it was wiped out at the Bighorn. They number 6,000 on their Montana lands.

Below: *A Crow delegation in 1880. Left to right, they are Old Crow and Medicine Crow, both of whom fought at the Rosebud in 1876, Two Belly (standing — but some doubt remains whether it really is him), Long Elk, Plenty Coups and Pretty Eagle. Plenty Coups is considered by most to be the greatest Crow chief.*

CROW

The Crow tribe were noted for their fine horse furniture. Note the rawhide and buckskin saddle with the horsehair rope (left) and the beautifully decorative beadwork for the horses chest. The stone–headed war clubs are typical of plains weaponry, as is the eagle feather headdress. Each feather would have been awarded for an act of bravery in war, known as a coup, which involved touching the enemy in one way or another. The peace medal (center) belonged to Plenty Coups. (Buffalo Bill Historical Center, Cody)

DELAWARE
North East
Also called Lenni Lenape ("True or Real Men") this major confederation of the Algonquian occupied an area from Cape Henlopen to Long Island, centered around the Delaware River basin. They were probably the most important Atlantic coastal tribe and had sub-tribes such as the Munsee, Unalachtigo and Unami. They were agriculturalists, hunters and fishers who moved west as guides and trappers for the whites. They ceded much of their land to William Penn in the 17th century (the first to indulge in this policy) and drifted onto territory of the hostile Iroquois. They moved west, eventually rekindling their alliance and confronting the expanding whites. (It was from among the Delaware that a prophet emerged in 1762 who inspired Pontiac of the Ottowa.) They proved their capabilities by defeating Braddock during the French and Indian War; raiding Ohio and Kentucky settlers in Lord Dunmore's War of 1774; opposing the Revolution; and then taking part in the defeat of St Clair in 1791 when over 600 US soldiers died in one battle.

Between 1778 and 1861 the Delaware had taken part in 45 treaties and —

thanks to alcohol, corrupt speculators, and a misguided relationship with the British — emerged with nothing, ceding only vast tracts of land. Today some 3,000 live in Oklahoma, Wisconsin (with the Stockbridge) and Ontario. A few mixed-bloods live on in part of their original lands. A traditional bark-painted history of the tribe exists called the Walum Olum.

DIEGUENO
California
These Yuman-speaking potters and basket-makers were named after the Franciscan mission of San Diego. They resisted the missionaries and attacked their missions but succumbed to them in the end. They consisted of a number of groups — the Kamia, Ipai, Tipai and Kumeyaay. Their culture reflected that of the Luiseno to the north and the Yuman Mojave to the east. Their religion involved a drug made from the toloache root which was used to seek visions. About 700 survive today.

Right: *Diegueno men in traditional feather headdresses and black-and-white body paint. The women wear plaid shawls, probably acquired from the mission.*

DUWAMISH
North West
This Coast Salish tribe had a chief who gave his name to the city of Seattle. They live now among their allies the Squamish at Puget Sound.

ERIE
North East

Often referred to as the Cat Nation these Iroquoian speakers lived in permanent stockaded towns on the south shore of Lake Erie and had a disastrous war with the gun-armed Iroquois League in 1653-6 which wiped them out as a separate unit.

ESSELEN
California

Hokan speakers who lived just to the south of the Costanoan. They were the first original Californians to become extinct, merging and disappearing into the Spanish missions at San Carlos.

EYAK
North West

An Athapaskan-speaking tribe from the extreme north west who served as middlemen in the copper trade between the Tlingit and the interior. They also separate the Pacific coast eskimos from the coastal Tlingit.

Right: *Flathead woman and young girl on horseback with lavish regalia. The woman has an infant's cradle attached securely to her horse's saddle pommel.*

FLATHEAD
Plateau

Often called Salish, the Flathead were very much of such stock but only one of the bands. They lived to the east in western Montana and thus resembled the tribes of the plains in terms of dress, customs, tipis and horses. Their name derived from the fact they did not practice deformation like their coastal relations. Their periodic pursuit of game in plains country led them into conflict with the Crow and Blackfeet — who they probably supplied horses to — during which they held their own. Due to their contact with converted Iroquois involved in the fur trade the Flathead became ready converts for the Christian missionaries seeking souls to save. Perhaps as a result, they did not go to war with the United States and ceded their lands peacefully during the 1850s in return for portions of their ancestral lands for their own use. Closely related to the Pend d'Oreilles and Kutenai, they live today with the latter on the Flathead Reservation in Montana where, combined, they number over 7,000 members.

FOX
North East

These central Algonquians from the forests of Wisconsin called themselves Mesquakie or Muskwakiwuk ("Red Earth People"). Like others, they lived in permanent summer villages and undertook communal prairie buffalo hunts in winter. They were notable for being one of the few woodland tribes to use the horse. A highly democratic society, they moved to Illinois, then dispersed to Iowa, Kansas and Oklahoma. They were enemies of the Sioux and Chippewa, and allies of the Iowa, Winnebago and Potawatomi. They fought the Americans and merged with the Sauk, or Sac, from Green Bay after their defeat in the Black Hawk War of 1832 during which the Sioux fought as auxiliaries for the US government. It is with the Sauk that the 1,500 Fox-Sauk are found today. The Fox are noted from their ribbonwork and it was from their ranks that the famous athlete Jim Thorpe emerged.

Right: *Wah-com-mo or Fast Walker, a high ranking Fox warrior, who wears a claw necklace, carries a pipe tomahawk, and sports a hair roach.*

GOSIUTE
Basin

Linked ethnically with the western Shoshoni and speaking a Ute language these people still live in the arid a Great Basin west of Great Salt Lake, an area of scarce food supply that led to a culture of respect for plants and animals capable of survival in the hostile environment.

GUALE
South East

Also known as the Yamasee these Muskogeans waged war against the white settlers in 1715 and were defeated. They fled to Florida where the Spanish called them Guale.

HAIDA
North West

Speaking an Athapaskan related language the Haida live on Queen Charlotte Island in British Columbia and to the south of Prince of Wales Island further north in Alaska where they are

Right: *Johnny Kit Elswa, a Haida from Skidgate Village, Queen Charlotte Island. The tattoos are his clan symbols — a bear on his chest and dogfish on each forearm.*

called Kaigani. They are related to the Tlingit and Tsimshian and are cultural-ly typical of tribes in this area: skilful carvers and carpenters, makers of giant cedar totem poles, fisheaters, and celebrators of potlatch ceremonies. The Haida were noted for their carving of argillite. Theirs was a highly ranked class society and their rituals involved the achievement of status by displaying and distributing wealth. This shocked whites and potlatches were banned from 1884 to 1951, an act intended to undermine Indian culture which nearly succeeded.

HALCHIDHOMA
South West
Hokan-speaking lowland Yumans (or Euqchans) living along the Colorado River and its tributaries. They were destroyed by internal warfare.

HAVASUPAI
South West
Rancheria farmers related to the Hualapai and Yavapai, the Hokan-speaking "Nation of the Willows" live in the upland region of north western Arizona in Cataract Canyon, near the Grand Canyon. They have adopted many Hopi traits.

HIDATSA
Plains
Linguistic cousins of the Crow, they are often called the Gros Ventre, Minitari, and Ree, but called themselves "The People of the Willows". They farmed the upper Missouri River, developing strains of maize still used today, and lived in villages of round, earth-roofed lodges. The women worked on the land while the men hunted and waged war. They were also involved as middlemen in much of the trading of guns to the west and horses to the east. They were close to the Mandan and like them were bad-ly affected by smallpox in 1837, losing half their 1,200 people.The survivors of the two tribes banded together after-wards at Fort Berthold in 1845 where they were joined in 1862 by the Arikara. In 1868 these became known as the Three Affiliated Tribes and there in North Dakota 5,000 remain to this day.

HOH
North West
Fishermen and neighbors of the Quinault and Quileute, this tribe has a tiny reservation in Washington bound-ed by the Hoh River and the Pacific Ocean. It is home to under 100 people.

HOPI
South West

This western pueblo tribe speak a Shoshonean language of Uto-Aztecan stock, thus making them closer ethnically to the Great Basin tribes than to their pueblo neighbors. The "Peaceful People" live in 11 terraced adobe pueblos and independent towns on three high mesas of the Colorado Plateau in north east Arizona. They have been in the area for perhaps 1,000 years and number 9,000 people. They were the only pueblo group to remain independent of the Spanish. Rich in ancestor myths they possess a powerful religious culture with elaborate ceremonies (including the famous Snake Dance and their kachina god-spirit representations) and are highly skilled craftsmen — notably their silver jewelery work.

Below: *Hopi men emerging from the men-only kiva. This underground chamber is a center of pueblo life and hosts secret ceremonial rituals.*

HOUMA
South East

A tribe of Muskogean language stock, they took in their kin the Acolapissa in 1750 and then the Choctaw-speaking Bayagoula. They are found today at Golden Meadow, Louisiana.

HUALAPAI
South West

Named the "People of the Blue-Green Water", the 1,000-plus Hualapai live in the heart of the Grand Canyon and have been there for 600 years. Their isolation has protected them.

HUPA
California

Living along lower Trinity River these Athapaskan speakers were culturally similar to the Yurok because of trade links. They share the White Deerskin, Brush and Jumping dances, and the World Renewal ceremony. They subsisted on salmon and acorns and lived in cedar plank houses. Their shamans were powerful people and tribal wealth was based upon dentalium shells and woodpecker scalps; their sense of value was highly developed. Today they have a reputation as fine basket makers.

Above: *A Hupa White Deerskin dance in 1891. The rice-stuffed deer heads are decorated with woodpecker scalps. Dances might last up to two weeks long.*

HURON
North East
An Iroquoian-speaking confederacy of four groups which totalled 20,000 before it was shattered by war with the Iroquois League in 1649. They had always been enemies and the situation worsened with the fur trade. This tribe lived along the St Lawrence River in Ontario, near Lake Simcoe, in longhouses. They were mainly crop growers and had named bands (Rock, Bear, Deer etc) formed from groups of villages. One-time allies of the French, they lost out in the Anglo-French struggle and were forced into migration by war, disease and pressure from white settlers. One group went west with the Petun and later became the Wyandotte. Dispossessed, the Huron took part in Pontiac's uprising in 1763 and like so many other tribes they are now found in Oklahoma.

ILLINOIS
North East
Another confederacy, this time of Algonquians, these hunting peoples were spread over parts of what are now called Wisconsin, Illinois, Iowa and Missouri and were first met by the French in 1667. Their main tribes were the Cahokia, Kaskaskia, Michigamea, Peoria, and Tamaroa. Under threat from raiding Sioux and Fox they concentrated in time along the Illinois River where they then were subject to the twin threats of aggressive Iroquois and French alcohol. Jesuit priests were also active among the Illinois. It was a Cahokian warrior who murdered Pontiac in 1769 and the Illinois suffered badly at the hands of the Sauk, Fox, Kickapoo and Potawatomi. Inevitably, they ended up in Oklahoma and are known now simply as the Peoria.

IOWA
Plains
The "Sleepy Ones" were the last Woodland Indian group to move to the plains and spoke a Siouan language called Chiwere. Reflecting this past, they lived in earth houses and only used tipis when hunting or waging war. Their warriors wore scalp locks, like the Kansa and Osage did. In 1836 they ceded their lands, having seen what happened to Black Hawk's Sauk, and moved to what are now Kansas, Nebraska and Oklahoma where today they total 1,000.

IROQUOIS
North East

This language group included the Huron and Cherokee, but the term mainly refers to a very important league formed around 1570 by five tribes in upper New York state. Tradition has it that Deganawidah and Hiawatha organized it under the "Tree of Great Peace" and all those neighbors who would not join became potential enemies. The principal member was the Mohawk, the others were Cayuga, Oneida, Onondaga and Seneca. It became the Six Nations around 1722 when the Tuscarora joined its ranks.

Of Woodlands culture, these tribes spread to the Appalachian highlands from their Great Lakes base. They lived in elm-bark covered longhouses in fortified villages and organized the league in a very democratic manner which may have influenced the US Constitution. Culturally, this matriarchal society was famous for its mask-making societies and wampum belts. They were feared because of their love of war (males were reared to show neither fear nor pain) and ritual torture of prisoners. Skilled diplomats, they played an influential role in the Anglo-French struggle for control

of the continent and once armed by the Dutch they crushed New France's allies, the Hurons, in 1648-50 in the so-called Beaver Wars and then fought the French for 30 years until 1690.

Despite having only 2,000 warriors they always tried to keep their autonomy from both colonial powers, but tended to favor the English. Their low point came with the War of Independence which split them, caused a civil war, and led to the loss of their lands in 1794. The

Above: *The six chiefs of the Six Nations of the Iroquois. The wampum belts they hold are mnemonic devices decorated with motifs symbolic of agreements and treaties with the white settlers.*

Cayuga and the pro-British Mohawk under Thayendanaga (Joseph Brant) mostly fled to Canada where they live today; the acculturated Oneida live mostly in Wisconsin; the other three remain in New York.

KALAPUYANS
North West
Ravaged by the epidemic of 1824 they moved onto the Grande Ronde reservation in Oregon with 13 other tribes in 1908, among them the Lakmiut.

KALISPEL
Plateau
The French traders called these Salish speakers from the valleys of northern Montana, Washington and Idaho the Pend d'Oreilles ("Ear Drops") because of their large, shell earrings. They were expert canoeists and often traveled to the plains to trade for hides. They live now on two Washington reservations — Colville and Usk.

KANSA
Plains
Living as hunters and farmers along the Kansas and Saline rivers this tribe, also known as the Kaw, spoke the Siouan dialect called Dhegiha. They wore scalp locks and were related to the Omaha and Osage but warred with them, as well as with the Fox, Pawnee and Cheyenne. In 1846 they were given a reservation in Kansas but in 1873 were removed to Oklahoma where 500 live today.

Above: *An elderly Karok in his war costume of rod armor and helmet with an animal-skin quiver of arrows.*

KARANKAWA
South West
This name was applied to a number of hunter-gatherer groups along the Gulf of Mexico. The French explorer La Salle was the first European to encounter them. Their decline began with the incursions of white settlers in the early 19th century. They fought with the Texans in the 1840s but were extinct shortly after, possibly hunted down because of their rumored cannibalism.

KAROK
California
The name is an adverb meaning "upstream" and describes their position in relation to the Yurok. They speak a Hokan language but share cultural traits with the Yurok. They prided themselves above all on their skilful shamen and are known for river platforms for salmon fishing.

KICKAPOO
North East
Algonquians living between the Fox and Wisconsin rivers who were kin to the Sauk and Fox tribes. Their name comes from the word Kiwigapawa, meaning "He Stands About". They absorbed the survivors of the Mascouten who the French had nearly wiped out. They were formidable warriors and followed Tecumseh in 1810, then fought with British forces against the Americans from 1813 to 1816. Let down by the British after the war, they were forced into a settlement to cede their lands and move to Missouri. In 1852 a large group moved to Mexico from Texas where they have a reservation. Today, the Kickapoo also live in Kansas and Oklahoma. They total over 2,000 people.

KIOWA
Plains

Aztec-Tanoan speakers who were among the last to accommodate the white settlers. There were six bands (just five remain) plus their kin in the Kiowa-Apache tribe. Former Crow allies, they moved from the Black Hills to Colorado in about 1805. They were warrior horsemen of some panache and led by great chiefs such as Lone Wolf, Kicking Bird, Satanta, and Satank. They were also very artistic. Together with their Comanche allies they spread the peyote religion, and with their allies they have shared territory in Oklahoma, situated between the Red and Washita rivers, since 1868. They are perhaps best known for their biannual pictographic summary of tribal events. These were painted on animal skins every winter and summer for over 100 years.

KIOWA-APACHE
Plains

A tribe long associated with the Kiowa but speaking an Athapaskan language similar to that of the Apaches, indicating they originated in the north. They ranged territory to the south of the Kiowa and were led by chiefs like Wolf Sleeve.

KITTANEMUK
California

Shoshonean stock people assimilated into the Californian mission culture.

Above: *Kicking Bird, the great warrior chief of the Kiowas. He tried to counsel peace with the whites and was poisoned for it by those favoring hostilities.*

KLAMATH
Plateau

The Eukshikni or ''People of the Lake'' managed to adopt the traits of three cultures (north west coast, Basin, and plains) due to their inter-tribal trading contact. They lived in Oregon — over 2,000 still do — and are related to the Modoc who share their Lutuami language.

KLIKITAT
Plateau

Sahaptin speakers from the Idaho-Washington area who acted as middlemen between the coast and inland tribes. Noted for their cedar-root baskets.

KOASATI
South East

Muskogean speakers from what is now called Alabama, some of whom moved to become the Coushatta of Louisiana and Texas. A little over 1,000 live in the two states today.

KONKOW
California

A major group of the Maidu language family (Penutian stock) decimated by disease by 1850.

KUTENAI
Plateau

Salishan speakers, a tribe to whom they are closely related. They lived in an area of British Columbia, Idaho and Montana and reflected plains and plateau cultures — fishing and canoeing like the plateau, dressing and living like the plains. They warred often with the Blackfeet, from whom they were probably descended. The 1,000 left today often work as guides and ranchers. They live on Flathead Reservation in Montana with the more numerous Salish.

KWAKIUTL
North West

One of the tribes lending their name to branches of the Wakashan language family, this British Columbia/Vancouver Island tribe was divided into three dialect groups — the Haisla, Heiltsuk and the southern Kwakiutl. They lived in large, wooden planked houses and held elaborate potlatches and had important dancing societies. They are famed for their elaborate totem carvings and dramatic, decorative wooden dance masks, made of cedar.

LAKES
Plateau

Also called the Senijextee they spoke the same language as the Okanagan and are a Salishan people. They live today as part of the 11-strong group of tribes on Colville Reservation at Nespelem, Washington.

LAKMIUT
North West

One of 14 tribes forming the confederation of Grande Ronde in Oregon.

LASSIK
California

Also known as the Wailaki these 1,000 Athapaskan speakers famed for beadwork live on Round Valley Reservation.

LUMBEE
South East

A post-colonial tribe that has evolved from a mixture of displaced Indian tribes. These North Carolinians contain Cheraw and Tuscarora blood.

Left: *Cedar plank houses and canoes typical of a Kwakiutl village, this one being Koskimo, at Quatsino Sound, Vancouver Island, in 1880.*

LUMMI
North West

Culturally strong Straits Salish tribe from Puget Sound in northern Washington state, traditionally known for basketry, weaving and carving. Like others in the area, they lived in cedar planked longhouses and ate much seafood; today the tribe operates its own fleet of fishing vessels.

MAHICAN
North East

An Algonquian (also called Mohican) tribe who inhabited parts of modern New England and would have met early European settlers, especially the English. James Fenimore Cooper's novel of 1826 traditionally immortalized the last of the tribe, and in 1991 it was made into yet another movie.

MAIDU
California

A large tribe of Penutian-speaking people, the Maidu's home was the area of the basin drained by rivers entering San Francisco Bay, northern California. Between 1899 and 1903, the anthropologist Roland B. Dixon assembled a fine collection of Maidu (including Konkow and Nisenan) artifacts; in their use of available natural resources they well illustrate Maidu economy and lifestyle.

MAKAH
North West

The Makah lived in large plank houses in five semi-autonomous villages on the tip of Olympic Peninsula. The potlatch, a ritualized dispensing of wealth, was a notable part of their culture, as was whale hunting, a prestigious and important occupation pursued in large sea-going canoes. Makah women contributed to tribal subsistence by gathering berries, shellfish and roots; the men were particularly adept at wood-carving.

Left: *A Makah fisherman with a whaling harpoon made of yew. This one is about 18ft (6m) long and has a cutting point of mussel shell.*

NAVAJO

These fine examples of Navajo material culture were collected between 1860 and 1900, the drinking cup and pouch (top right) of c.1869 being the earliest pieces.

Long known for their silver jewelry, Navajo of the last century could be receptive to outside influences: as an interesting example, the shape of the crescent necklace pendants with hands

— known as naja — came to the Navajo, from among whom it was collected in 1893, via Moslem North Africa, Spain, then Mexico. (Smithsonian Institution, Washington DC)

MALISEET-PASSAMAQUODDY
North East
Two tribes speaking the same eastern Algonquian language and split by the modern Canadian/US border. Some of the first to come into close contact with Europeans, they were also among the most decimated or dispersed tribes in the north east.

MANDAN
Plains
Siouan-speaking farmers, the Mandan lived in earth lodges on the Missouri River. They were beautifully captured by the Swiss painter Karl Bodmer in the 1830s. Sadly, Bodmer was only just in time to record a culture in despair: in 1837 the greater part of the tribe was wiped out by the white man's smallpox virus.

MARICOPA
South West
A Yuman-speaking tribe who, along with other rancheria groups such as the Mohave and Tarahumara in the south west, occupied settlements along rivers or in well-watered mountain and desert regions in southern Arizona and New Mexico.

MASCOUTEN
North East
An Algonquian-speaking tribe whose lands edged Lake Michigan; by 1800 they had lost their identity through merging with neighboring tribes, notably Kickapoo, Fox and Piankashaw.

MASSACHUSET
North East
In the early 1600s this tribe suffered defeats at the hands of the Micmac, who were aided by superior weapons supplied by French colonists. By 1640 their numbers had been reduced by disease and deprivation from about 3,000 (in 1600) to less than 500.

Above: *A Menominee winter dwelling in the traditional style, a domed wigwam framework of bent saplings covered with mats of reeds and cattails.*

MATTAPONY
North East
Formerly in the Powhatan confederacy, this tribe now lives on a reservation near West Point, Virginia.

MENOMINEE
North East
One of a group of central Algonquian tribes clustered around the Great Lakes, the Menominee lived on the north banks of modern Lake Michigan in the Green

Bay area. (Today the tribe still lives on a reservation in the same region.) They depended on horticulture for subsistence, harvesting (though not cultivating, for religious reasons) the nutritious aquatic plant generally called wild rice. The tribal name derives from the Chippewa for wild rice, *manomini*.

MIAMI
North East
An Algonquian tribe living on the south of Lake Michigan, allies of the Mascouten, Kickapoo and Potawatomi. They participated in Pontiac's War of 1763 in which the Ottawa chief laid siege to the fort at Detroit (which he failed to take).

MICMAC
North East
The Micmac still live in areas of Nova Scotia (early name Acadia) and New Brunswick that they occupied in the 16th century and before. Living in heavily forested regions with many lakes and rivers, their dependence on the use of birch bark was considerable. During the French period (1600-1760) fur trapping for trade transformed Micmac life, but

contact with the English thereafter confined them to reservations and destroyed the old hunting and fishing economy forever.

MISSION
California
A generic term given to those Indians of California who grouped around Catholic missions. They include the Cupeno, Diegueno, Fernandeno, Gabrielino, Juaneno, Luiseno, Salinan and Serren.

MISSISSAUGA
North East
A Chippewa band who lived in southern Ontario. As did many northeastern tribes they sold off traditional lands to English and Canadians. One such cession in 1784 saw about three million acres sold in return for "£1,180 in goods".

Below: *A Micmac home of poles and branches bound with cedar bark fiber and covered with overlapping birch bark and grass matting.*

MISSOURIA
Plains
Merged with the Oto in the early 1800s; speakers of a Siouan language. Along with others of this language group such as the Kansa, Iowa and Osage they were part hunters, part farmers, living with a degree of permanency in earth covered lodges.

MIWOK
California
Speakers of a root of the Penutian language, this group of N. Californian tribes includes Miwok, Lake Miwok and Coast Miwok. They lived east and north of San Francisco. Coast Miwok are said to have welcomed the Englishman Sir Francis Drake and his crew in about 1579. Their womenfolk practiced tattooing, body painting and wore clothing adorned with the feathers of many different birds. Clamshell disk beads were also worn but more usually served as currency.

MOBILE
South East
One of the tribes, usually grouped with their neighbors the Tohome, which resisted the Spaniard Hernando de Soto

Above: *Captain Jack. His executed body became a fairground attraction.*

when he crossed their lands, 1539-43. This was a disastrous episode for de Soto but a far worse one for the Indians: hundreds were kidnapped and killed, thousands died thereafter of diseases introduced by the invaders. Both Tohome and Mobile spoke a variety of the Choctaw language, with whom they fused in about 1770.

MODOC
Plateau/California
Hunter-gatherers whose boundaries ran across our own geographical areas, the Modoc people are well known for their spirited resistance to the US Army under the leadership of Kintpuash, known to the whites as Captain Jack, in 1872-3. History tells of the siege of the Lava Beds (1873) and Modoc repelling of US cavalry, infantry, artillery and militia, the murder of Brigadier General Canby and Captain Jack's final capitulation, capture and sentencing to death. His remaining 153 Modoc were relocated to Indian Territory, in present-day Oklahoma. They were allowed to return to the Klamath Reservation in 1909.

MOHAVE
South West
Yuman speakers, the Mohave are one of the rancheria peoples who, at the time of Spanish contact, formed some of the largest agricultural groups in the south west. They lived along the Colorado River. The family was an important unit in Mohave life; in the 1850s a family would have lived in a scattered rural setting in a log house roofed with thatch and covered with sand.

MOHAWK
North East

The Mohawk called themselves "The Possessors of the Flint". Speakers of the Northern Iroquoian language, they were farmers and fishermen yet often lived in fortified villages. One of the five primary tribes who founded (in 1570) the Iroquois League, its purpose to establish and secure peace and to acquire strength to resist aggressors. In this they were known as "guardians of the eastern door". Benjamin West's famous 1771 painting "The Death of Wolfe" depicts a tattooed Mohawk warrior beside the fallen British general, for whom he had been fighting, after the capture of Quebec in 1759.

MOHEGAN
North East

A New England tribe (Connecticut) often linked with the Pequot, with an economy based on the cultivation of maize and on hunting and fishing. Both tribes were jointly ruled by the Pequot chief

Right: *A Mohawk girl, stagenamed White Deer, wearing idealized traditional dress for New York's Pan-American Exposition which took place in 1901.*

Sassacus in the early 17th century until a rebellion of the Mohegan sub-chief Uncas led his people to independence. After the destruction of the Pequot in 1637, most came under Pequot control, but continued white settlement gradually displaced the Mohegan themselves.

MOLALA
Plateau

Poorly recorded tribe of the Penutian family, neighbors of the Klamath and Tenino, their lands also bordered those of the Northern Paiute.

MONO
Plateau/California

A group name for some of the tribes known as "Digger Indians" because of their habit of digging for root plants (where they were not too rare) in their inhospitable desert environment.

MONTAUK
North East

An Algonquian-speaking Long Island tribe, not the best placed to resist incoming colonists. In 1784 Mohegans and Montauks moved to a tract of land received from the Oneidas (of the Iroquois people).

NAKIPA
South West
Yuman-speaking tribe of northern Baja California, neighbors of the Paipai.

NANTICOKE
North East
Atlantic coast group, formerly inhabiting parts of present-day Delaware and Maryland; from 1642 to 1678 they were in constant dispute with Maryland colonists. Algonquian speakers, the major part of the group migrated to join Iroquois in the 1720s.

NARRAGANSET
North East
An important Algonquian New England tribe (Rhode Island) who, with other Atlantic coastal tribes (Penobscot, Pequot, Wampanoag), fought bloody battles against English settlers. King Philip's War (1675-6) largely destroyed the Narraganset. Canonchet was a notable and brave Narraganset leader who died at the hands of the English.

NATCHEZ
South East
Numbering about 4,500 in 1650, the survivors of a 1731 French attack were eventually amalgamated with the Creeks and Cherokees. The language is an isolate, not known to be related to another one. The Natchez had an elaborate social system, which included two classes, nobility and commoners. The highest ranking chief was known as the Great Sun (nobility); when he died his wives (commoners) were sacrificed so as to be able to accompany his spirit to the afterworld. The Natchez were descendants of the temple mound builders.

NAVAJO
South West
Calling themselves the Dineh (People), the Navajo are today the largest N. American Indian tribe in population and in area of reservation lands. They are notable for their artistry, producing fine rugs and blankets and silver jewelry. Sand paintings are a part of their curing ceremony. Of the same Southern Athapaskan group as the Apache (they were, indeed, Apacheans), they too suffered in their contact with the US Army. The infamous Long Walk (1864), a forced march undertaken by men, women and children to imprisonment in Fort Sumner in New Mexico, was a pivotal event in their history.

Above: *Showing the influence of the plains, this mounted Nez Perce warrior wears an eagle feather warbonnet. The tipi is made of canvas.*

Left: *A Navajo war captain posing with lance and shield at Keam's Canyon, Arizona, in winter 1892-3. Although sedentary sheepfarmers, the Dineh were also fierce warriors.*

NEUTRAL
North East

Iroquoians neutral in the wars between the Huron and Iroquois, inhabiting lands between lakes Huron, Erie and Ontario. Iroquoians of the Five Nations (before the Tuscarora made it Six) turned savagely upon the Neutrals after they humanely gave shelter to beleaguered Huron; the Neutrals never recovered.

NEZ PERCE
Plateau

Notable horsemen who adopted a number of Plains traits and developed the sturdy Appaloosa horse, the Nez Perce were also famous for their superb cornhusk bags. They are more tragically known for the brave resistance of Non-Treaty Nez Perce in the late 1870s to the cession of their ancestral lands (by Treaty Nez Perce) to the US Government after gold was discovered. Refusing the treaty, Chief Joseph (Hein-mot Too-ya-la-kekt) and five other band chiefs fled with their followers to the buffalo country of Montana, evading pursuit and capture by the US Army until they were caught just short of the Canadian border and safety. Some 150 Nez Perce were then settled in a reservation in Washington state. Joseph died broken hearted. Meeting some Nez Perce early in the century, Lewis and Clark had regarded them as being ''among the most amiable people we have seen''.

NICOLA
Plateau

Small northern Athapaskan band of the high plateau, neighbors of the Shuswap, Thompson, among others.

NIPISSING
North East

A tribe of eastern Ontario, with an Algonquian culture identifying them with the Chippewa.

Below: *Nuu-chah-nulth men and women outside their ceremonial house showing goods obtained from trading, such as the blanket and firearm.*

NIPMUC
North East

Little-known Algonquians of central Massachusetts, but one of the tribes which participated in, and was virtually destroyed by, King Philip's War (1675-6).

NISENAN
California

Northern Californian, but the southernmost branch (living along the Sacramento River) of what, until the turn of the century, were called Maidu.

NOMLAKI

Northern California tribe, speakers of a root of the Penutian language, as the Maidu, Wintu, etc.

NOOTKANS
North West

Nowadays also called Nuu-chah-nulth, Nootka being a name given them by the Englishman Captain James Cook, and closely related to the Makah. Inhabitants of the west coast of Vancouver Island, they are well-known for their artistic, unconventional wood-carving skills. These include ceremonial masks and headdresses. They were also notable whale hunters.

OFO
South East

Speakers of a Siouan language, the Ofo were driven south from the Ohio River area by the expanding Iroquois.

OJIBWA (PLAINS)
Plains

Algonquian speakers linguistically related to the Blackfeet, Plains Cree, Gros Ventre. They were one of a group of woodland Indians who, gradually forced out of their original homelands, adapted to the horse culture of the plains.

OKANAGAN
Plateau

Salishan speakers of the northern Plateau, the Okanagan were typical travelers to the great trading fairs of the region such as occurred at The Dalles, Kettle Falls and Celilo Falls. Like the Shuswap and Thompson, they retained the canoe as a primary means of transport in a land of fast-running rivers and streams. Their canoes were especially notable for being of the "sturgeon-nose" type — sharp snouted and made of cedar bark — a style used by Coeur d'Alêne and Kutenai.

OMAHA
Plains

Speakers of a Siouan language, the Omaha of the Lower Mississippi frequently warred with the Sioux who also raided other near relatives — Crow, Iowa, Mandan — as well as the Omaha. One of a number of plains tribes to which warrior societies were important; in the case of the Omaha these were age-graded, and introduced boys early to the belief in the war ethic.

ONEIDA
North East

A northern Iroquoian linguistic group of the St Lawrence lowlands who practiced intensive horticulture and fishing. Their name for themselves translates as ''The People of the Standing Stone'', after a granite boulder near their former village. One of the tribes of the Five (later Six) Nations and representatives of the Tuscarora on the Council of Six, they were loyal to the French rather than the British. They also fought for the Americans in the War of Independence (1775-83). Some migrated to the Thames River, Ontario, after that war, others to a reservation on Green River, Wisconsin.

Above: *An Onondaga chief holds wampum strings during a tribal meeting in 1910. Note the flags of the deer and turtle clans. The Union Jack and royal portraits perhaps suggest the tribe's pro-British roots.*

ONONDAGA
North East

'The People on the Hills', an important Iroquois tribe of the Five Nations whose translation of their name referred to the position of their principal village, which was also the capital of the confederacy. The Onondaga were considered ''keepers of the council'' and ''keepers of the wampum'', the latter being tribal belts of great symbolic importance which recorded treaties and agreements between whites and Indians.

OOWEKEENO
North West

One of numerous coastal tribes, neighbors of the Bella Coola and Kwakiutl, who benefited from the bountiful sea life and temperate climate of the Pacific coast.

OPATA
South West

A Piman-speaking culture, language related to that of the Tarahumara, inhabiting the rugged interior of Chihuaha and Sonora. The Spanish, and later Mexican, policies of concentrating small nomadic bands (such as the Opata) in Chihuaha led to the consolidation and extinction of many groups. By the mid 1700s, the Opata were indistinguishable from the Spanish or Mexican population.

OSAGE
Plains

Speakers of a Siouan language, part farmers, part hunters (deer, buffalo), with a lifestyle similar to that of the Omaha, Iowa, Kansa etc. During the 1920s the Osage enjoyed, it is said, the greatest income per person of any individual group in the world, this as a result of realizing (some of) the oil wealth of their land in Oklahoma (Indian Territory). The Osage nonetheless suffered enormously at the hands of corrupt, and corrupting, whites in this period. The prominent Osage Washin-ha was the foremost spokesman for his tribe during this time of wealth. His splendid regalia and items of ceremonial importance reside in the Smithsonian Institution.

OTO
Plains

Another Siouan-speaking tribe, essentially farmers, of the Lower Mississippi. One of many tribes eventually moved to Indian Territory by the whites.

Left: *Utse-tah-wah-ti-an-kah of the Osage in an otter skin turban and holding a magnificent war club — a weapon typical of the middle-Missouri tribes.*

OTTAWA
North East

Algonquian speakers of the Great Lakes region. Friendly with the French, under whose missionary influence they fell, and after the destruction of the Huron they were often attacked by the Iroquois. Pontiac was the most notable Ottawa chief; he rallied Indians in Pontiac's War (1763) against the English invaders. His organization of tribes north west of the Ohio River ultimately failed to capture the forts at Detroit and Pittsburgh; gradually abandoned by his Indian allies, Pontiac was eventually murdered in St Louis. His heroic belief in his people marks him as one of the greatest leaders of the Indian nation.

PAIPAI
South West

Also called the Akwa'ala, the Paipai are Yumans, a generic term for River Yuman tribes (such as Cocopa, Havasupai etc) living along the Gila River, in northern Baja California.

Right: *Oto warriors. The central figure carries a long pipe with a head of red catlinite stone, much prized among tribes of the plains region.*

PAIUTE
Basin
Includes Northern (Paviotso), Southern (Chemehuevi) and Owens Valley Paiute, all Shoshonean speakers. With Gosiutes, Panamint and others, the Paiute represented a particular culture sustained in and around the arid Great Basin region for thousands of years. They used a wide range of plant and animal (deer, mountain sheep) resources, fruit, seeds and especially the pinon (pine nut), which was collected in finely woven baskets in whose production they excelled. The Great Basin religion put strong emphasis on immortality and in 1889 Wovoka, a Paiute holy man, had a vision, the influence of which was to spread to the Plains in the form of the Ghost Dance.

PALUS
Plateau
Like their near neighbors the Umatilla, the Palus of the Columbia River were heavily influenced by plains tribes after the "Equestrian Revolution" (in which horses were introduced) of about 1750. Skilled horse-breeders, it is possible that the name Appaloosa, a horse normally associated with the Nez Perce, derives from their name. They were speakers of the Sahaptin dialect.

PAME
South West
The southernmost of tribes in this designated area, bordering Middle America, the Pame were early beneficiaries (1750s) of the work of the Spanish missionary Junipero Serra who built five missions, some still in use, and introduced the Pame to agriculture and animal husbandry.

PAPAGO
South West
Known today by their name Tohono O'Odham (Papago, translating as 'bean eaters', is considered derogatory), one of the agricultural rancheria Piman-speaking groups residing in Arizona, south of the Gila River and west of Tucson.

PATWIN
California
Northern Californian tribe, with the Konkow, Nisenan etc, speakers of a root of the Penutian language. Formed a part of California's flourishing native culture before the old ways were swept away.

PAWNEE
Plains

One of the principal Caddoan tribes and probably the first to arrive on the Plains (moving into Nebraska from east Texas in the 1300s), the Pawnee lived in more or less permanent earth lodges in villages along the Platte River. The Morning Star and Evening Star became strong elements in their cosmic view of the universe, and they observed a ritual ceremony around the former which demanded human sacrifice. In the 1820s Petalesharo, a young Pawnee, saved a sacrificial victim from death and thus changed the course of the ceremony in the future. The Pawnee claimed never to have fought the US Government, generally, as in the Indian Wars of 1865-85 (in which they fought as uniformed scouts) fighting with the Army against other Indians. Another Petalesharo (II) was instrumental in maintaining good relations with the whites. He was murdered by one of his own people when he opposed their movement to Oklahoma. Despite their loyalty to the whites it was a fate they could not avoid. Forced off their lands onto Indian Territory, half of the Pawnee died of disease and exposure.

Above: *A typical Pawnee village of earth lodges. This is a ceremony at Loup Fork, Nebraska, in 1871.*

PENOBSCOT
North East

With the Passamaquoddy, the only large Indian group still living in New England (Maine). Speakers of the Algonquian language.

PEORIA
North East

A tribe of the Illinois confederacy of Indians who were eventually settled in north east Oklahoma with Senecas, Ottawas etc. In the 18th century the (French) Jesuits were active among the Peoria and in time the Wea and Piankashaw of the Miami Indians were absorbed into their ranks.

SIOUX

Perhaps no tribe epitomizes the plains Indians more than the Sioux, and the men's artifacts here are, in their use of feathers, beads, quills, deer and buckskin, redolent of the plains culture. Particularly fine is the buckskin shirt (left), with beaded panels and fringes of human hair at the neck and arms. The war shield (top right) is rawhide, centrally adorned with the carcass of a bird of prey, with hawk feathers and horsetail attached. Note also the exquisite moccasins decorated with seed beads which cover the soles. (Buffalo Bill Historical Center, Cody).

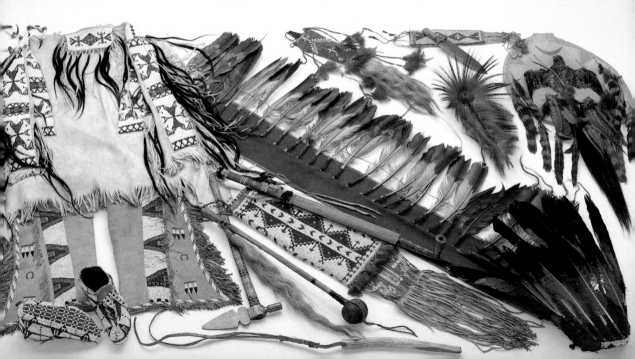

PEQUOT
North East
One of the numerous tribes who fought the English colonists of Connecticut and Massachusetts. In the Pequot War of 1637 the Pequot were deliberately destroyed by English Puritans and their Mohegan and Narraganset allies, the pre-dawn massacre of a village on the Mystic River being the nadir of this unrestrained violence. Some Pequot warriors were enslaved and sent to the West Indies in exchange for black slaves, who became the first from those colonies to appear in New England. Some survivors of the Pequot still, however, live in Connecticut.

PERICÚ
South West
Former inhabitants of land on the southernmost point of Baja California, neighbors of the Guaycura.

PETUN
North East
One of three Iroquoian tribes (with the Neutral and Erie) based around lakes Ontario and Erie, they were destroyed by Iroquois of the Five Nations between 1649 and 1656. Some survivors were adopted by the Iroquois or joined the refugee Huron. They were also called Tobacco Indians, for obvious reasons.

PIANKASHAW
North East
Formerly a sub-tribe of the Miami. When the Miami chief Little Turtle defeated American forces in 1791, his people suffered as a consequence, ultimately finding homes in Oklahoma and becoming divided into three groups, one of which was the Piankashaw.

PIMA
South West
The Pima name for themselves is O'Odham (the People). Pima may be divided into four groups — River Pima, Papago (Tohono O'Odham), Pima Bajo and Sobaipuri. The latter group lived in south east Arizona and were driven out by Apache and Spanish, then intermingled with other Piman groups. All Piman groups were agriculturalists: River Pimans supplied food for the Union Army during its western campaigns during the Civil War. River Pimans also served in the war on the side of the Union in Arizona Territory, and also scouted in the Apache Wars.

Above: *A Pima woman from the Gila River Reservation in Arizona. She has her face painted in the traditional manner of the tribe.*

They remember the bleak "Forty Years of Famine", suffered by their people as a consequence of their rivers being diverted by Anglo settlers, as a result of which their crops were denied water and starvation ensued.

POMO
California

No other American Indians match the Pomoan tribes for their extraordinarily skilled basket weaving techniques which used different types of materials that might include roots, bark, leaves, reeds and feathers. Such techniques as "three-strand braiding" put them ahead of other Californian tribes in terms of sophistication and application of natural resources. Exquisite examples of Pomoan basket work gathered by the anthropologist J.W. Hudson in the late 1880s/1890s are held at the Smithsonian Institution. Hokan speakers of at least six distinct languages, the main Pomoan bands were North Western, Central, Southern, South Eastern and Eastern Pomo, living in an area north of San Francisco and especially on the Russian River and around Clear Lake.

PONCA
Plains

Speakers of the Siouan language Dhegiha, the Ponca lived on the Lower Missouri. They were neighbors of the Omaha and Pawnee. Moved out of their South Dakota/Nebraska homelands in the 1870s to Indian Territory.

Above: *Famous Pomo basket maker Joseppa Beatty working at her home on the Yokayo Rancheria in 1892. This is a one-rod coiled design.*

POTAWATOMI
North East

Algonquian speakers, closely related to the Ottawa and Chippewa (Ojibwa), who occupied the lands hemmed in by lakes Michigan and Huron. During the colonial wars they sided with the French against the English, then with the English against the Americans. Following American independence, the homelands of the Potawatomi and their neighbors would be snapped up by land hungry whites. Around 1820 they started to withdraw across the Mississippi and onto reservations on Oklahoma and Kansas, where the Potawatomi Indian Reservation stands today, north of Topeka, Kansas.

POWHATAN
North East

A large Algonquian confederacy with their homeland between the Potomac and James rivers on the eastern seaboard. The name Powhatan is attributed to the chief of the confederacy whose daughter Pocahantas married the English settler John Rolfe of Jamestown, thus forming a firm relationship between whites and Indian of the region. Without the help of the Powhatans, the English settlers would not have survived their first bitter winter of 1607-8. Friendship did not endure: by the 1640s tribal power, including that of the Powhatans, had been broken forever by ever encroaching colonists.

PUEBLO
South West

Aptly named by the Spanish who first encountered them, the pueblos are not tribes but village-based autonomous political units (almost theocracies) whose peoples live in multi-chambered stone or adobe houses. Of special interest in pueblo culture is the half-underground, sacred, ceremonial chamber, known as the kiva, where men carry out secret rituals.

There are four language groups (Tanoan, Keresan, Zuni and Uto-Aztecan) and two main divisions based on location and ecological adaptation: the Eastern is the largest and uses irrigation agriculture because of the pueblos' proximity to the Rio Grande; the Western are skilled dry farmers. The 19 New Mexico pueblos have a rich cultural life and cling to their independence fiercely. (Counting the Zuni and adding Ysleta pueblo in Texas brings the total to 21.) The Eastern has five Keresan pueblos — Cochití, Santa Ana, San Felipe, Santo Domingo, and Zía. The Tanoan-speakers are split into six Tewa pueblos (Nambe, Pojoaque, San Ildefonso, San Juan, Santa Clara, and Tesuque), four Tiwa (Isleta, Picurís, Sandía, and Taos)

and one Towa (Jémez). The Western has two Keresan pueblos, Acoma and Laguna, a Tewa group associated with the Hopi who are known as the Hano, plus the Hopi and Zuni themselves who are very distinct peoples (see separate entries).

The modern-day pueblos (excluding Hopi and Zuni) have a population of about 20,000. They produce excellent pottery and jewelry, often of a style distinct to a pueblo, and their dances and festivals are major events and attractions.

Above: *Cochití pueblo, in the Eastern division, in the late 1870s. Visible (right) is corn drying on the rooftops of this ancient pueblo, which dates to the middle of the 13th century.*

QUAPAW
Plains

Like the Poncas, speakers of the Siouan language Dhegiha and inhabitants of the Lower Missouri. They were one of the smaller groups that shared Indian Territory with the Five Civilized tribes (Choctaw, Cherokee etc).

QUECHAN
South West

A Yuman-speaking society living along the Colorado River. Also known as Yuma. One of a number of tribes (including Yana, Karok etc) to which the name Hokan has been given.

QUILEUTE
North West

Coastal dwellers and renowned whale hunters, their homeland was to the south of Vancouver Island.

QUINAULT
North West

A Salish tribe met by Lewis and Clark living along the Pacific coast between the Quinkate and the Quaitso to the north, the Chehalis to the south. Salmon fishers along the river of the same name, they lost much of their land due to its rich timber resources.

SANPOIL
Plateau

Like the Flathead, Coeur d'Alêne etc, the Sanpoil were Salishan speakers. They lived in parts of present-day Washington state and Idaho, along the Columbia River. Located in the center of the Plateau, they lived in a form of cultural isolation from their neighbors. The Sanpoil believed in equality for all within the tribe.

SARCEE
Plains

Athapaskan speakers of the northern plains, this small tribe, as with the Gros Ventre, allied with the Blackfeet (Algonquian speakers) during the 19th century. They originally came to the plains from Canada.

SAUK
North East

Also known as Sac, an Algonquian tribe closely related to the Fox (see also Fox), with whom they formed a close alliance in the 1730s, although maintaining their own identities. Black Hawk and Keokuk (Kiyo' Kaga) were two renowned leaders of the Sauk. Black Hawk sided with the English against the Americans in 1812; in 1832 he fought, and was defeated by, the US Army over the sales of Sauk lands east of the Mississippi. This is known as the Black Hawk War. Many Sauk (and Fox) were thereafter moved to lands in Kansas. Keokuk was an outstanding orator. He went to Washington to contest claims of the Sioux over lands occupied by the Sauk and Fox — and won. A man who understood the futility of resisting the inevitable advance of the frontier, he died in 1848, poisoned it is said by one of his own people. Perhaps not everyone approved of his philosophy. A bronze bust of Keokuk stands in the Capitol in Washington, DC.

Left: *Keokuk, the Sauk leader famed for his oratory, pictured in 1846-7, shortly before his death.*

SEMINOLE
South East

The Seminoles were descendants of Creek colonists who migrated from the northern regions of the south east into Florida in the 18th century. They split into two distinct but related language groups, the Muskogee and the Mikasuki, this occurring after the Americans destroyed the Creek confederacy in the Creek Wars (1813-14). In the 1820s and 1830s many Seminoles — along with Cherokees, Choctaws, Chicasaws, Creeks — were deported under great duress to Indian Territory. The Trail of Tears was aptly named. In their new land these tribes reorganized and re-established themselves and became known as the Five Civilized tribes. George Catlin painted a well-known portrait of the Seminole leader Osceola, who led the resistance of some of his people to movement from their Florida homelands. His stand provoked a 7-year guerrilla war against the US Army, which the latter did not win. After Osceola's capture and death (1838) some Seminole chiefs agreed to move to Indian Territory; others did not and remained in their Everglades fastness, "the tribe which never surrendered".

SENECA
North East

Northern Iroquoians, one of the founding tribes and the westernmost of the Iroquois League. Their names for themselves were "The Great Hill People" and "Keepers of the Western Door". The War of Independence not only broke the League but it saw the destruction of many Seneca villages by American forces who objected to their neutrality. There are today three Seneca reservations in western New York state — the Allegany, Cattaraugus and Tonawanda. On each of them stands a ritual structure associated with the Longhouse religion founded by the Seneca prophet Handsome Lake early in the last century.

Left: *This man wears traditional Seminole men's clothing, probably from the turn of the century, or later. Note the (left) shoulder belt, generally of woven beadwork, falling to and knotted at his right hip, with tassels.*

Right: *Interior of a Shoshoni lodge, 1878. The woman standing has a fine trade item, a striped Witney 'point' blanket. Beaded saddle bags are indications of an equestrian people.*

SERI
South West

Like the Chemehuevi, the Seri were one of the tribes who lived in the extremely marginal environment on the fringes of the south west culture area, on the arid coast of Sonora, Mexico. They grew none of their own food but lived a hunter-gatherer existence, subsisting on small game and marine and desert products. They lived in a nomadic and semi-nomadic life in small family groups and bands.

SHASTA
California

A northern California tribe belonging to the Hokan linguistic family. They had regular contact with the Karok, trading deerskins, obsidian (a volcanic rock resembling bottle glass) and sugar-pine nuts to the Karok for baskets, canoes, dentalium shells and seaweed.

SHAWNEE
North East

Algonquian speakers and one of the most important tribes of the north west Ohio country from the mid-18th century, although their former lands were around the Cumberland River in Tennessee. Tecumseh was the foremost Shawnee leader who envisioned a great Indian state in the Ohio valley, and one which could be achieved by an uprising of united tribes. However, defeat by the Americans at the Tippecanoe River in 1811 undid his plans. When war broke out between the English and the Americans, Tecumseh sided with the former, organizing an Indian brigade. He died fighting the Americans, probably a disillusioned man but a great orator and leader of his people. The Shawnee eventually moved to Oklahoma.

SHOSHONI
Basin

A Shoshonean-speaking people, including the Eastern Shoshoni, Northern Shoshoni and Bannock and the Western Shoshoni. After 1840 the Northern Shoshoni and Bannock had to venture onto the plains to hunt buffalo, thus bringing themselves into contact with more hostile tribes. Washakie (of the Wind River Reservation, Wyoming) born when the Missouri country was still unexplored, was a diplomatic and experienced Shoshoni leader of noble repute. Allied with the United States in the Indian Wars of the 1870s, he served General George Crook in his plains campaigns. Washakie understood the futility of resisting white progress and accepted the inevitability of reservation life. He died in 1900 and was buried at Fort Washakie.

SHUSWAP
Plateau

Salishan speakers and the northernmost Plateau tribe with lands around the Fraser River in British Columbia. Like the Thompson and Okanagan, the Shushwap lived in semi-subterranean earth lodges.

SIOUX
Plains

The Sioux nation (Siouan speakers) of the central plains was originally divided into three parts, forming the Dakota (Santee), Nakota (Yankton) and Lakota (Teton). The Teton crossed the Missouri for the central plains, also becoming known as the Western Sioux. They consisted of seven sub-tribes — Brule, Hunkpapa, Miniconjou, Oglala, Oohenonpah/Two Kettle, Sans Arc and Sihasapa/Blackfoot. Nomadic hunters who followed the buffalo (which supplied most of their basic needs), the Sioux lived in lodges (tipis), simple conical structures originally constructed of lodgepole pines and buffalo skins. Exquisite Sioux art is represented by quill work (made from flattened porcupine quills) which decorated mocassins, shirts, leggings etc, and much later, beadwork.

Crazy Horse (Tasunke Witco) was perhaps the finest, certainly the most enigmatic, warrior-commander of the Lakota. A decoy at the Fetterman fight (1866), he fought the Army with notable success at the battles of the Rosebud and Little Bighorn. In 1947 a sculptor, Korczak Ziolkowski, began to shape a statue of Crazy Horse on Thunderhead

Mountain in the Black Hills. Although the sculpture is still unfinished, visitors may today see the strong image of Crazy Horse emerging from the granite mountains of his homeland. Sitting Bull (Tatanka Yotanka) and Red Cloud

Above: *The prolific Edward Curtis photographed this Hunká-Alowanpi Ceremony of the Oglala Sioux in 1907; among the Lakota it was associated with the mythological figure of the White Buffalo Maiden.*

Above: *Gall (also called Pizi and The Man Who Goes in the Middle) was a Hunkpapa leader of prodigious strength and bravery, especially at the Little Bighorn. It is said that he died on George Custer's birthday.*

(Mahpiya Luta) of the Hunkpapa and Oglala were noble leaders of their people. Red Cloud fought the US Army to a standstill in the 1860s; Sitting Bull's role before and after the Little Bighorn (1876) is well documented. His assassination in 1890 and the subsequent massacre at Wounded Knee on the Pine Ridge Reservation are sorry episodes — which still reverberate — in the history of whites-Indians relations. Today there are reservations at Pine Ridge and Standing Rock, among others.

SKOKOMISH
North West
"The River People" are Salishans living at the mouth of the Salish River in Washington state, where they have a reservation.

SPOKANE
Plateau
With the Flathead, Coeur d'Alêne etc, one of the well-known Interior Salish (and Salishan-speaking) tribes of British Columbia and Washington. The Spokane Reservation today occupies lands on the eastern side of the Columbia River.

SUSQUEHANNOCK
North East
Northern Iroquoians living along the Susquehanna River in Pennsylvania and New York, they were conquered by the Iroquois in the 1670s and then absorbed into the Five Nations.

SWINOMISH
North West
Also known as the Southern Coast Salish and Puyallup, their lives were changed dramatically by the infiltration of non-Indians into the Northwest Coast territory of today's Washington state.

TAKELMA
California
A tribe culturally similar to the Shasta of northern California, they were involved in the Rogue River War of 1855-6 and afterwards sent to the Siletz Reservation.

TENINO
Plateau
Speakers of the Sahaptin dialect and inhabitants of part of modern Oregon, east of the Willamette River, which today includes their present home, the Warm Springs Reservation.

THOMPSON
Plateau

Speakers of a Salishan language, the Thompson Indians live in British Columbia, east of the Coast Range. When whites first arrived (1858-9) they were living in villages along the Thompson, Fraser and Nicola rivers. In their rugged homeland their winter houses were large, semi-subterranean earth covered structures; in the summer they lived under a mat covered framework of poles. The ethnographer James Teit collected fine examples of Plateau tribes material culture at the end of the century, including that of the Thompsons, some of which is housed in the American Museum of Natural History, New York.

TILLAMOOK
North West

A once prominent Salishan-speaking tribe of northwest Oregon. In the early 19th century they occupied some eight villages, with a population of about 2,200. By the 1850s that number had been reduced to about 300.

Right: *Tlingit potlatch dancers, some wearing Chilkat blankets, at Klinkwan, Alaska, in about 1900.*

TLINGIT
North West

The Tlingit are a nationality inhabiting the strip of mainland and the hundreds of islands along the coast of southeastern Alaska. Separate tribes include Hutsnuwu, Chilkat, Hoonah, Stikine among others. The Tlingit were masters of working cedar wood. The houses were of course wood, as were food boxes and bowls, eating implements, hats and masks. Many of these objects were decorated in the so-called "Northern formline" style, which entailed the "wrapping" of painted or carved two-dimensional forms around three-dimensional objects. The treasured Chilkat blanket (part of dance and feast regalia), made by women from mountain goat wool and cedar bark, also featured this particular style, generally showing elaborate figures.

TOLOWA
California
Athapaskan speakers and northernmost coastal group whose name derives from their dialect. Considered by their neighbors the Yurok to be quite wealthy, the Tolowa traded in dentalium shells (acting as middlemen) which came from Vancouver Island. They were also skilled boatmen, constructing canoes from the wood of redwood trees.

TONKAWA
Plains
In the 19th century allies of the Apache and enemies of the Comanche. For some years after Texas was annexed (1845), Tonkawas, Caddos and Pehnatekuh Comanches, all of whom found themselves without agents or reservations, suffered greatly at the hands of the Texans.

TSIMSHIAN
North West
Skilled wood-carvers and neighbors of the Haida of Queen Charlotte Island, with whom they shared a two-dimensional art form so similar also to that of the Tlingit that the two are often indistinguishable.

TUNICA
South East
Numbering some 2,500 in 1650, less than 50 survived in 1910. Their language, although well recorded, is not known to be related to another.

TUSCARORA
North East
Iroquoian speakers whose names for themselves were "The Hemp Gatherers" and "The Shirt Wearing People". Formerly dominant inhabitants of North Carolina, after ruinous defeats by whites and their Indian allies in 1811-13, many moved north to join the Iroquois League making the Five Nations *six*, probably between 1715 and 1722. Some, however, remained on a reservation in Bertie County, North Carolina, until 1803, when they joined other Tuscaroras who had previously moved to a reservation near Niagara Falls, New York state.

TUTELO
South East
Speakers of a Siouan language, they numbered some 2,700 in 1600; by 1800 the descendants had joined the Iroquois in Canada.

UTE
Basin
Shoshonean speakers, the Utes inhabited the valleys among the mountain ranges of central and western Colorado and parts of Utah. They formed three main divisions — the Uintah, Yampa and Uncompahgre. The Utes acquired horses — using them first as pack animals — as early as 1650.

Below: *Part of a Ute encampment in the Wasatch Mountains, Utah, in about 1873. The tipi is made of elk skin.*

WAMPANOAG
North East

Algonquian speakers of the eastern seaboard (Massachusetts, Rhode Island). Massasoit of the Wampanoag allowed English colonists to settle; his son Metacomet — or King Philip — lent his name to the war of 1675-6 which saw the power of the New England tribes destroyed by the colonists.

WAPPINGER
North East

The name given to some minor Algonquian tribes of western Connecticut and New York's Hudson River valley.

WAPPO
California

A tribe with a language (Yukian) related to the Yuki, their near neighbors. Parts of the Wappo land were surrounded in a small enclave by the more numerous Eastern and South Eastern Pomo.

WASCO
Plateau

Like the Wishram, speakers of a Chinookan dialect who lived in the vicinity of The Dalles, the site of the great Rendezvous on the Columbia River.

WASHOE
Basin

A small tribe from the Great Basin which lived around Lake Tahoe and spoke a language unrelated to others.

WENRO
North East

Iroquoian speakers inhabiting the southern shores of Lake Ontario who took refuge with the Neutrals (their western neighbors) from the Iroquois.

WICHITA
Plains

Like the Pawnees, who they followed onto the plains after 1300, speakers of the Caddoan language, and inhabitants of Texas. The Spanish explorer Coronado is said to have visited the Wichita in 1541. Some Wichita now live in Oklahoma.

WINNEBAGO
North East

The only speakers of the Siouan language (much like that of the Oto, Iowa and Missouri of the plains) in a predominantly Algonquian-speaking area. Inhabitants of southern Wisconsin, they were forced to move to Nebraska in the 1870s. However, some returned, so that Winnebagos now live in the old and new homelands.

Left: *Blackhawk and Winneshiek, two prominent leaders of the Winnebago in the 1870's land struggles*

TLINGIT

Although the superb mountain goat's wool Chilkat blanket catches the eye in this spread, other artifacts suggest the richness of the lands where the Tlingit lived (Pacific coast with dense forests behind) and their use of natural resources and symbols. The three carved wooden boxes (top) held food; another wooden food dish (right, across the blanket) is in the shape of a seal; and the wooden hat (top left) is carved with beaver and potlatch rings. The dance cape under the hat has fringes tipped with deer hoofs. (Smithsonian Institution, Washington DC)

WINTU
California

Hill people of northern California whose economy was based on salmon, deer and acorns. The Wintu suffered greatly from the effects of white incursion — among them a malaria epidemic in the 1830s caused by gold miners polluting their streams; the introduction of cattle ranching; massacres and forced relocation. After the arrival of the railroad in 1875 their culture changed even more dramatically. The Wintu made fine and artistic baskets, many of them collected by Livingston Stone in the McCloud River region from 1872 to 1875, and now housed in the Smithsonian Institution, Washington, DC.

WISHRAM
Plateau

Members of the Chinookan family and inhabitants of land between the Columbia and Willamette rivers.

WIYOT
California

A north California coastal tribe (neighbors of the Mattole, Nongatl) with a language remotely related to that of the Algonquian family.

YAKIMA
Plateau

Like the Nez Perce, to whom they were culturally similar, the Yakima were speakers of the Sahaptin dialect. Coming into contact with white explorers in the early 1800s, the Yakima also came to own horses, developed large herds and made forays onto the plains, adopting many of the habits of plains tribes.

YANA
California

Like the Karok, Shasta, Yuki, Pomo and Yuma, the Yana were of Hokan stock (Hokan being the base of their dialect). Their lands abutted that of the Wintu and Nomlaki, among others, in northern California.

YAQUI
South West

Cahitan speakers (like their southern neighbors the Mayo) and one of the rancheria groups. Although the Spanish were in early contact with such rancheria tribes, they never truly overcame the likes of Apache, Upland Yumans, Tarahumara or, indeed, the Yaqui. The Yaqui lived along the Yaqui River in Sonora, Mexico.

Above: *Lucy Thompson, a Yurok, also known as Che-na-wah as well as Weitch-ah-wah. She wears a basket cap and her extensive ornamentation points to her being a woman of wealth.*

YAVAPAI
South West
An Upland Yuman tribe, culturally similar to the Havasupai, who once inhabited western and northern Arizona, regions which lacked enough water for permanent farming. Thus they were more hunter-gatherers than agriculturalists. Through extensive intermarriage and because of enforced internment on Apache reservations some Yavapai became intermingled with Western Apache but by 1910 many had begun to drift from the San Carlos Apache Reservation back to their traditional homelands.

YOKUTS
California
Hunter-gatherers of central California, of whom the Northern Valley, Southern Valley and Foothill Yokuts were the most prominent, speakers of a root of the Penutian language.

Right: *Zuni Bow Priests en route to visit the Seneca in the East, taken in 1882 by John K. Hillers who worked extensively for Cushing during this period. Hillers also photographed at Zuni Pueblo.*

YUCHI
South East
A tribe originally in the Appalachian highlands, they numbered about 1,500 in 1650; by about 1930 only 200 remained among the Creeks (with whom they shared cultural similarities) in Oklahoma after their removal together in 1836. The Yuchi language is an isolate, unrelated to any other.

YUKI
California
Inhabitants of the northern California coast and of Hokan stock, but, like the Wappo, speakers of Yukian.

YUROK
California
A northern California tribe, speakers of a language remotely related to Algonquian, who lived on the lower Klamath River. The Yurok lived in more than 50 autonomous hamlets and were hunter-gatherers and fishermen, benefiting from the bounty of both river and ocean.

ZUNI
South West
The Zuni are puebloans who form, with the Hopi, Hopi-Tewa (Hano), Acoma and Laguna, the Western pueblos. They live in a large pueblo in northwestern New Mexico and speak a language unrelated to any other in the south west. Zuni pueblo has been occupied for at least 600 years and despite interaction with Spaniards and Mexicans it has always maintained its independence. Like other puebloans, the Zuni have rich cultural traditions; their exquisite silver and turquoise jewelry and pottery are artforms that express their view of the world, which is, simply put, that man must live in harmony with nature. Smithsonian ethnologist Frank Hamilton Cushing made extensive and valuable studies of the Zuni in the early 1880s.

Index

Entries in *italics* refer to illustrations